D0049372

Happy Thoughts

333 Things to Make You Happy

By Suzanne Beilenson
& Lisa Berman

Designed by Michel Design

PETER PAUPER PRESS, INC.
WHITE PLAINS · NEW YORK

To the cast of thirtysomething

Copyright © 1991
Peter Pauper Press, Inc.
202 Mamaroneck Avenue
White Plains, New York 10601
ISBN 0-88088-282-4
Printed in Hong Kong
7 6 5 4 3 2 1

Happy Thoughts

333 Things That Can Make You Happy

1. Balancing your checkbook on the first try

2. A warm fire on a winter night

3. Getting a refund check from the IRS

4. Getting into a bed with clean sheets

5. Waking up and nothing hurts

6. When Monday Night Football starts an hour early

7. Watching the perfect sunset with the one you love

8. Coming home and finding 6 messages on your answering machine

9. Finding money in a public telephone

10. Catching a train just as it's about to pull out

11. The smell of pine in the woods

12. Getting bumped up to First Class

13. Having clear skin for three days

14. The sound of the ocean

15. Eating homemade brownies

16. Getting a good haircut

17. Having people tell you you look thinner

18. Getting an air mail letter

19. Getting an extra hour of sleep when the clocks are set back

20. When your boss goes on vacation

21. When you go on vacation

22. Getting the answer on Final Jeopardy

23. Winning two dollars on a Scratch and Win ticket

24. Winning $2 million in the State lottery

25. Finding a good bathing suit

26. Clean underwear

27. Getting a present that you like
    from your grandmother

28. A good night's sleep

29. Getting your braces removed

30. Hearing your favorite song on the radio

31. Having a good horoscope

32. Running into your old boy/girlfriend when you're looking good

33. Getting a free pay cable station

34. Chocolate chip cookie batter

35. A kiss from a small child

36. A hand-knit sweater made for you

37. Fridays

38. Rainy Sunday mornings

39. Snowdays

40. When your newborn baby sleeps through the night

41. Finding a bouquet of flowers waiting on your doorstep

42. Agreeing on a video to rent with your friend

43. Having an empty seat in front of you at the movie theater

44. Being the last one to get tickets to a play

45. A good cup of coffee

46. Waking up before your alarm goes off

47. Coming home and finding someone did the dirty dishes you'd left in the sink

48. Waking up early and realizing it's Saturday

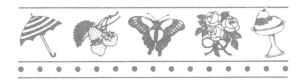

49. Trick-or-treating

50. Making all the green lights

51. Remembering your keys

52. Corn-on-the-cob

53. Hot cocoa with marshmallows

54. A peanut butter and jelly sandwich

55. A hot fudge sundae

56. Getting a promotion

57. Being tucked into bed

58. Making a deadline

59. Being in the middle of a good book

60. New sneakers

61. Speaking a foreign language

62. Finding your way with a map

63. Discovering a good new restaurant

64. Being the first stop on a crowded elevator

65. Making resolutions you can keep

66. Identifying a new bird you've never seen before

67. Hearing good gossip

68. A new lipstick

69. Finding out you get President's Day
off when you didn't think you would

70. Eating lunch when you've skipped
breakfast

71. Having an umbrella when it's not
supposed to rain—and it does

72. A hug when you really need one

73. Figuring out how to use your new computer

74. Fresh-squeezed orange juice

75. Making up with your boy/girlfriend

76. Finding a long-lost earring

77. A brand new tube of toothpaste

78. Flossing your teeth

79. Getting into the college of your choice

80. Winning an argument

81. Playing football on Thanksgiving

82. Driving around the neighborhood
    to see the Christmas lights

83. Taking an outdoor shower in the sun

84. Hearing a cat purr

85. Fireworks on the Fourth of July

86. Walking in the rain

87. Chocolate milk

88. Having your cast taken off

89. Getting a perfect score on a test

90. Getting the window seat on an airplane

91. Being met at the train station/airport by someone you love

92. A good slice of pizza

93. When the leaves turn colors

94. The first snowfall of the season

95. Oiling a squeaky door

96. Growing vegetables

97. Picking vegetables out of your own garden

98. Flying a kite

99. Eating outside/picnic in the park

100. Feeling a crewcut on a small boy

101. Playing with puppies

102. A good photograph of yourself

103. Scratching an itch

104. Completing everything on your list of things to do

105. Having cold champagne for an unexpected celebration

106. Walking barefoot in the grass

107. Thanksgiving leftovers

108. Spaghetti on a fork

109. Dinner with friends

110. Running through sprinklers

111. Licking batter off beaters

112. Watching ducks cross a road

113. Wading in a fountain

114. A string quartet

115. A candlelit dinner

116. Eating when you're really hungry

117. Looking out the window on a train ride

118. Watching your favorite team win
     the Super Bowl/Stanley Cup/
     World Series

119. Having someone cook you dinner

120. Watching kindergarteners at nap time

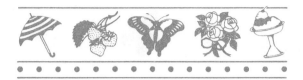

121. A hot shower after a workout

122. A massage

123. Hitting a home run

124. Catching a touchdown pass

125. Breakfast in bed

126. Having someone fetch the Sunday paper for you

127. Leftover birthday cake for breakfast

128. Laughing so hard you cry

129. Running into an old friend on the street

130. The Cha-Cha

131. French fries and ketchup

132. Cold beer/drink on a hot day

133. Sun tea

134. Running into your ex boy/girlfriend
when you're with a new one

135. Toasting marshmallows over
an open fire

136. Sleeping late

137. A walk in the woods

138. Skinny-dipping

139. Having a shirt pressed

140. Coca-Cola from a glass bottle

141. Eating ice cubes

142. Sprinkles on an ice cream cone

143. Having someone brush your hair

144. A good fortune in a fortune cookie

145. Eating off someone else's plate

146. Staying at a hotel

147. Thick-pile carpeting

148. Hitting the ball on the sweet spot

149. Throwing a perfect spiral

150. Standing under a waterfall

151. Getting the right results on an
     early pregnancy test

152. The Sunday comics

153. A three-day weekend

154. Having a snowball fight

155. Making angels in the snow

156. Sledding

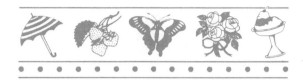

157. Twenty-One/Blackjack

158. When the dentist tells you
you have no cavities

159. Turning a double play

160. Getting box seats at the ball game

161. Catching a fly ball

162. Indian summer

163. Jumping in a big pile of leaves

164. GORP

165. Hiking to the mountain's peak

166. Sleeping under the stars

167. Telling stories by a campfire

168. People-watching

169. Reading a bedtime story out loud

170. Having your car washed

171. When the elevator is waiting for you

172. Riding in a convertible with the top down

173. Singing *Take Me Out to the Ballgame* in the seventh inning stretch

174. Holding hands

175. A cashmere sweater

176. Getting three seats across all to
     yourself on an airplane

177. Being on a highway when there's
     a big tie-up in the other direction

178. A hot bath

179. Apple cider on a Fall day

180. Figuring out "whodunnit" way
     before you get to the end of the book

181. Picking the right-sized container
to put the leftovers in

182. Catching a rerun of something
you missed

183. Threading a needle on the first try

184. Threading a needle on the fifth try

185. Going to see *The Nutcracker*
at Christmas

186. Watching a parade

187. Taking a small child to the circus

188. Cotton candy

189. Getting a check in the mail

190. Being on time

191. Getting dressed up for a
     special occasion

192. Going to a football game

193. A pair of old jeans

194. Gift-wrapped presents

195. Hearing church bells

196. Winning a bet

197. Getting a postcard

198. Getting an overseas phone call

199. Eating leftovers straight out of the fridge

200. Crackerjack prizes

201. Hot chocolate-chip cookies and milk

202. Finding a perfect shell at the beach

203. Waking up and realizing it was just a bad dream

204. Driving and singing along to the radio

205. Warm clothes out of the dryer

206. Seeing a falling star

207. Finishing the crossword puzzle

208. An old flannel shirt

209. A new box of tissues

210. Going through a day of work without snagging your pantyhose

211. Knowing where the candles/flashlight are when there's a blackout

212. Fresh-baked warm bread

213. Not buying a dress because it's too expensive; going back later and finding it on sale in your size

214. Catching the bouquet at a wedding

215. Getting a box of assorted chocolates, taking a bite out of some of them, and putting them back

216. Sipping iced tea on a porch on a hot day

217. Thinking you're eating ice cream and it turns out to be frozen yogurt

218. Making ice cream in an old-fashioned ice cream maker

219. Getting through customs quickly

220. A coffee maker that turns itself on before you get up

221. Fitting the last piece in a jigsaw puzzle

222. Getting a singing telegram

223. Petting the baby animals at the zoo

224. Finding out your friend taped
your favorite TV show you thought
you missed

225. A shopping spree on your mother's
credit card

226. Finding a parking spot in front
of the store you're going to

227. Eating popcorn at the movies

228. Watching *The Wizard of Oz*

229. Sailing a catamaran in the wind

230. Feeding sugar cubes to a horse

231. Getting up on water skis for the first time

232. A warm bed on a cold night

233. Going home early from work

234. Waking up and everything works

235. Fresh towels

236. Seeing your favorite old movie
on the big screen

237. Little kids on a playground

238. When the radio plays "our song"
and you and your boy/girlfriend
are together

239. Buying your first car

240. Buying your first new car

241. Letting a balloon fly away

242. Liking your blind date

243. Your teddy bear

244. Ice sculpture

245. Stained glass windows

246. Finding an antique you like
     at a garage sale

247. Hearing a baby's first words

248. Department store windows
at Christmas

249. Bowling a strike in the last frame

250. Shooting par

251. Building your own bookshelves

252. Fixing your car yourself

253. Guys playing saxophones

254. Finger painting

255. Picking wildflowers

256. A flock of birds heading South

257. The first robin of spring

258. A new dress

259. When you lose your wallet and someone calls to tell you he found it

260. Cinnamon toast

261. Wind chimes in an ocean breeze

262. When your teacher is absent

263. Calling your grandparents

264. A first kiss

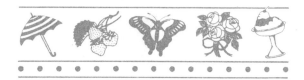

265. Your first swim of the summer

266. A beautiful day for an outdoor wedding

267. Passing your road test on the first try

268. Getting a frosting flower on your piece of birthday cake

269. Sandwiches with the crusts cut off

270. Apple-picking

271. Recycling your newspapers

272. Giving up aerosol spray cans

273. Being able to do 50 sit-ups

274. Blowing bubbles

275. A bonfire on the beach

276. Kissing under the water

277. Taking a shower after a day at the beach

278. Earning a free game on a pinball machine

279. Finding out that someone you have a crush on has a crush on you

280. When the guy/girl you met on vacation calls you at home

281. Diamonds on any occasion

282. Having a boy/girlfriend on Valentine's Day

283. When your luggage is the first to come out at the baggage claim

284. Waking up to a sunny day after a week of rain

285. Finding a penny on the street

286. A baby's smile

287. Waking up next to the one you love

288. Having your sunglasses with you when it's sunny

289. Getting an invitation to a party

290. Buying a plant and having it
survive the month

291. Seeing a great movie

292. Taking a long lunch hour

293. Coasting down a big hill after
having biked up it

294. Getting your pictures back from
your vacation

295. Catching a fish for the first time

296. Shelled pistachio nuts

297. Winning a tie-breaker in tennis

298. Wearing a new outfit and getting compliments on it

299. Serving an ace

300. Seeing a credit balance on your Visa or Mastercard bill

301. Ordering from a mail-order catalog
in the middle of the night

302. Not having to wait on line at the
Department of Motor Vehicles
or the bank

303. Getting a care package

304. Seeing your favorite painting in
a museum

305. Knowing the night before what
you're going to wear to work
the next day

306. Running a marathon

307. Curling up in bed with a good book

308. Soaking in a bubble bath

309. Lots of previews before the movie starts

310. Getting lots of phone calls on your birthday

311. Drinks on the house

312. Paying your last student loan installment

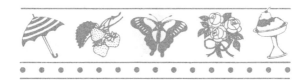

313. Getting your first real job

314. When your birthday wish comes true

315. Not owing anybody money

316. Having enough quarters to do
your laundry

317. Quitting a job you hate

318. A down comforter on a cold night

319. Your first formal

320. Making a seven-letter word in *Scrabble*

321. Winning a game of *Trivial Pursuit*

322. Having exact change for the toll booth

323. Getting to your parked car just as you're about to get a ticket

324. Having your cat curl up on your lap and fall asleep

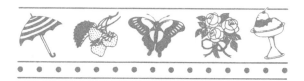

325. Finishing the Sunday paper
before Wednesday

326. Seeing a rainbow

327. Having nothing wrong with your
car on its 6-month checkup

328. Planning a surprise party where
no one gives away the secret

329. Getting paid without having to
ask for your check

330. Finding money in your coat pocket
left there last winter

331. Seeing the first crocus of spring
     poke through the snow

332. Looking at funny pictures in
     your high school yearbook

333. Going to a school reunion and
     looking younger and better than .
     your old boy/girlfriend

Things That Make Me Happy!

_____

_____

_____

_____

_____

_____

_____

_____

_____

_____

_____

_____

_____

_____

_____

Things That Make Me Happy!

_____

_____

_____

_____

_____

_____

_____

_____

_____

_____

_____

_____

_____

Things that make Me Happy!

_____

_____

_____

_____

_____

_____

_____

_____

_____

_____

_____

_____

_____